To _____

Peace

From _____

Peace

Illustrated by
JUDY PELIKAN

A Welcome Book

Stewart, Tabori & Chang
Publishers, New York

Published in 1994 and distributed in the U.S. by
Stewart, Tabori & Chang, 575 Broadway,
New York, New York 10012

Produced by Welcome Enterprises, Inc.
575 Broadway, New York, New York 10012
Text Research: Sally Seamans, Shannon Rothenberger

1 3 5 7 9 10 8 6 4 2
Printed in Italy

*Grateful acknowledgment is made to the following for permission to
reprint previously published material:*

Ulysses by James Joyce. Copyright © 1914, 1918 by Margaret
Caroline Anderson and renewed 1942 and 1946 by Nora
Joseph Joyce. Reprinted by permission of Random House, Inc.

"Peace" by Sara Teasdale. Reprinted with permission of
Macmillian Publishing Company from *Collected Poems of Sara
Teasdale* by Sara Teasdale (New York: Macmillan, 1937).

"A Certain Peace" from *My House* by Nikki Giovanni.
Copyright © 1972 by Nikki Giovanni. By permission of
William Morrow & Company, Inc.

Excerpt from *Memoirs* by Pablo Neruda, translated by Hardie
St. Martin. Translation copyright © 1977 by Farrar, Straus &
Giroux, Inc. Reprinted by permission of Farrar, Straus &
Giroux, Inc.

T is more than silence after storms. It is as the concord of all melodious sounds . . .

WILLIAM E. CHANNING

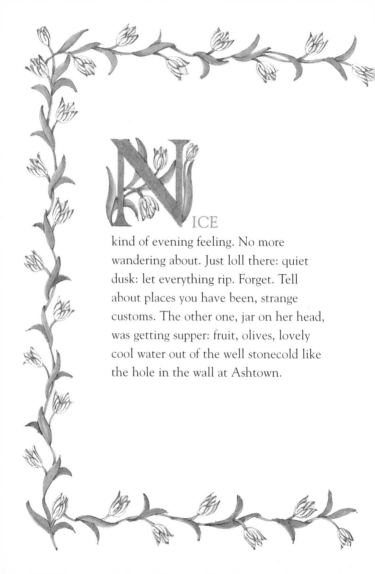

N

ICE kind of evening feeling. No more wandering about. Just loll there: quiet dusk: let everything rip. Forget. Tell about places you have been, strange customs. The other one, jar on her head, was getting supper: fruit, olives, lovely cool water out of the well stonecold like the hole in the wall at Ashtown.

MUST carry a paper goblet next
time I go to the trottingmatches. She
listens with big dark soft eyes. Tell her:
more and more: all. Then a sigh: silence.
Long long long rest.

JAMES JOYCE
Ulysses

I T

rains down
sounding
like someone
crinkling a caramel
corn wrapper
against
my window
i listen
lying
half asleep.

CATHY STEELE

THESE

roses under my window make no reference
to former roses or to better ones; they are
for what they are; they exist with God
today. There is no time to them. There is
simply the rose; it is perfect in every
moment of its existence. Before a leaf-bud
has burst, its whole life acts; in the
full-blown flower there is no more; in
the leafless root there is no less.

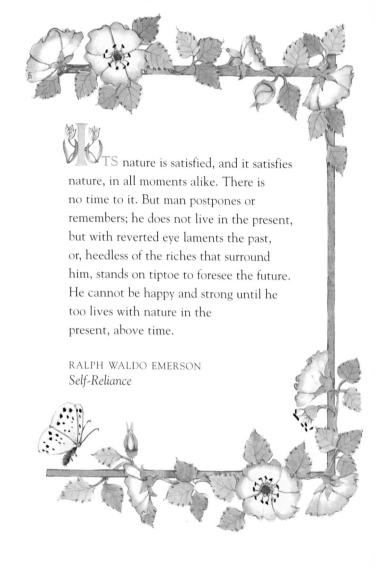

ITS nature is satisfied, and it satisfies
nature, in all moments alike. There is
no time to it. But man postpones or
remembers; he does not live in the present,
but with reverted eye laments the past,
or, heedless of the riches that surround
him, stands on tiptoe to foresee the future.
He cannot be happy and strong until he
too lives with nature in the
present, above time.

RALPH WALDO EMERSON
Self-Reliance

I will arise and go now, and go to
    Innisfree,
And a small cabin build there, of clay
    and wattles made:
Nine bean-rows will I have there, a
    hive for the honeybee,
And live alone in the bee-loud glade.

And I shall have some peace there,
    for peace comes dropping slow,

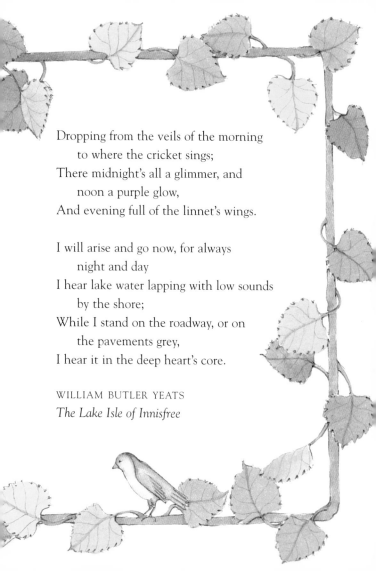

Dropping from the veils of the morning
    to where the cricket sings;
There midnight's all a glimmer, and
    noon a purple glow,
And evening full of the linnet's wings.

I will arise and go now, for always
    night and day
I hear lake water lapping with low sounds
    by the shore;
While I stand on the roadway, or on
    the pavements grey,
I hear it in the deep heart's core.

WILLIAM BUTLER YEATS
The Lake Isle of Innisfree

PEACE

flows into me
    As the tide to the pool by the shore;
    It is mine forevermore,
It will not ebb like the sea.

I am the pool of blue
    That worships the vivid sky;
    My hopes were heaven-high,
They are all fulfilled in you.

I am the pool of gold
    When sunset burns and dies—
    You are my deepening skies;
Give me your stars to hold.

SARA TEASDALE
Peace

it was very pleasant
not having you around
this afternoon

not that i don't love you
and want you and need you
and love loving and wanting and
    needing you

but there was a certain peace
when you walked out the door
and i knew you would do something
you wanted to do
and i could run
a tub full of water
and not worry about answering the phone
for your call

and soak in bubbles
and not worry whether you would
    want something
special for dinner
and rub lotion all over me
for as long as i wanted
and not worry if you had a good idea
or wanted to use the bathroom

and there was a certain excitement
when after midnight you came home
and we had coffee
and i had a day of mine
that made me as happy
as yours did you

NIKKI GIOVANNI
A Certain Peace

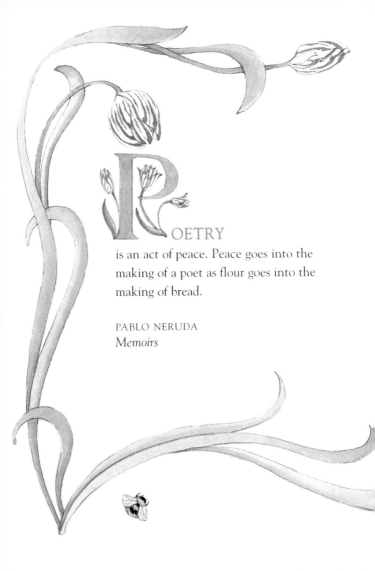

POETRY

is an act of peace. Peace goes into the making of a poet as flour goes into the making of bread.

PABLO NERUDA
Memoirs

A musician must make music, an artist must paint, a poet must write, if he is to be ultimately at peace with himself. What a man can be, he must be.

ABRAHAM HAROLD MASLOW
Motivation and Personality

CHANCE

pushed the heavy glass door open and
stepped out into the garden. Taut branches
laden with fresh shoots, slender stems
with tiny sprouting buds shot upward.
The garden lay calm, still sunk in repose.
Wisps of clouds floated by and left the
moon polished. Now and then, boughs
rustled and gently shook off their drops of
water. A breeze fell upon the foliage and
nestled under the cover of its moist leaves.
Not a thought lifted itself from Chance's
brain. Peace filled his chest.

JERZY KOSINSKI
Being There

DAYS

tumbled on days, I was in my overalls,
didn't comb my hair, didn't shave much,
consorted only with dogs and cats, I was
living the happy life of childhood again. . . .
I was as nutty as a fruitcake and happier.
Sunday afternoon, then, I'd go to my woods
with the dogs and sit and put out my hands
palms up and accept handfuls of sun boiling
over the palms.

JACK KEROUAC
The Dharma Bums

OVER
all the mountaintops
Is peace.
In all treetops
You perceive
Scarcely a breath.
The little birds in the forest
Are silent.
Wait then; soon
You, too, will have peace.

JOHANN WOLFGANG VON GOETHE
Wanderers Nachtlied

TOWARD

calm and shady places
I am walking
on the earth.

CHIPPEWA SONG

ROP

Thy still dews of quietness,
    Till all our strivings cease;
Take from our souls the strain and stress,
And let our ordered lives confess
    The beauty of Thy peace.

JOHN GREENLEAF WHITTIER

ONE world at a time.

HENRY DAVID THOREAU

HARRIET

had reached the cork tree. By standing
very quietly under it, she could hear the
woodpeckers tap-tapping on it far above
her head. She put her head back and
looked through the break in the branches
and their canopy to the sky, and as she
looked, the clouds, and the grey line with
a stone daisy that was the parapet of the
house, and the tall tree itself, seemed to
tilt gently backwards. "That is the world
turning," thought Harriet.

T gave her a large feeling to see the
tilt of the world. Clouds, house, tree,
lawns, river, Harriet, were borne slowly
backwards as the world turned, but the
tree remained upright, steady, rising into
the sky, spreading its branches that were
coming into bud. Under Harriet's feet,
where she stood among the red lilies, its
roots went deep into the earth, down
down into the pit of the earth.

RUMER GODDEN
The River

LAST

night, as I was sleeping,
I dreamt—marvelous error!—
That I had a beehive
here inside my heart.
And the golden bees
were making white combs
and sweet honey
from my old failures.

ANTONIO MACHADO

WHEN

despair for the world grows in me
and I wake in the night at the least sound
in fear of what my life and my children's
     lives may be,
I go and lie down where the wood drake
rests in his beauty on the water, and
     the great heron feeds.

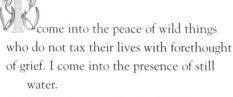

I come into the peace of wild things
who do not tax their lives with forethought
of grief. I come into the presence of still
water.
And I feel above me the day-blind stars
waiting with their light. For a time
I rest in the grace of the world, and am
free.

WENDELL BERRY
The Peace of Wild Things

TIS
the gift to be simple,
'Tis the gift to be free,
'Tis the gift to come down where we
    ought to be,
And when we find ourselves in the
    place just right,
'Twill be in the valley of love and delight,

W HEN

true simplicity is gain'd,
To bow and to bend we shan't be
asham'd,
To turn, turn will be our delight
'Till by turning, turning we come round
right.

SHAKER HYMN

BETWEEN the woods the afternoon
Is fallen in a golden swoon,
The sun looks down from quiet skies
To where a quiet water lies,
    And silent trees stoop down to trees.
And there I saw a white swan make
Another white swan in the lake;
And, breast to breast, both motionless,
They waited for the wind's caress . . .
    And all the water was at ease.

A. A. MILNE
The Mirror

HOME

at last and now it was the time she had
been looking forward to all week: fire-
escape-sitting time. She put a small rug
on the fire escape and got the pillow from
her bed and propped it against the bars.
Luckily there was ice in the icebox. She
chipped off a small piece and put it in
a glass of water. The pink-and-white
peppermint wafers bought that morning
were arranged in a little bowl, cracked,
but of a pretty blue color.

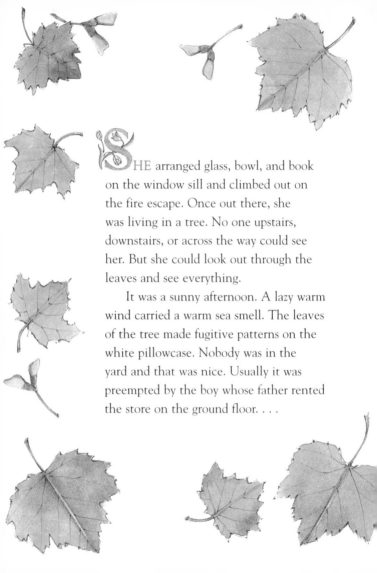

SHE arranged glass, bowl, and book on the window sill and climbed out on the fire escape. Once out there, she was living in a tree. No one upstairs, downstairs, or across the way could see her. But she could look out through the leaves and see everything.

It was a sunny afternoon. A lazy warm wind carried a warm sea smell. The leaves of the tree made fugitive patterns on the white pillowcase. Nobody was in the yard and that was nice. Usually it was preempted by the boy whose father rented the store on the ground floor. . . .

FRANCIE breathed the warm air, watched the dancing leaf shadows, ate the candy and took sips of the cooled water in-between reading the book. . . .

As she read, at peace with the world and happy as only a little girl could be with a fine book and a little bowl of candy, and all alone in the house, the leaf shadows shifted and the afternoon passed.

BETTY SMITH
A Tree Grows In Brooklyn

Y OU

are a child of the universe no less than the trees and the stars; you have a right to be here. And whether or not it is clear to you, no doubt the universe is unfolding as it should. Therefore be at peace with God, whatever you conceive Him to be. And whatever your labors and aspirations, in the noisy confusion of life, keep peace in your soul. With all its sham, drudgery, and broken dreams, it is still a beautiful world.

Desiderata

HAT

you are seeking is here.

HORACE